PRAYERS & DEVOTIONS
that
Change Lives and Hearts

Brenda R. Cox

authorHOUSE®

AuthorHouse™
1663 Liberty Drive
Bloomington, IN 47403
www.authorhouse.com
Phone: 833-262-8899

Published by AuthorHouse 01/19/2022

ISBN: 978-1-6655-4514-3 (sc)
ISBN: 978-1-6655-4523-5 (e)

I dedicated this book to the Peace of God that passes all understanding, which has kept me through the trials and tribulations of my life. The toughest one occurred when my mother, Brenda Crockett-Wood, transitioned to her Heavenly home in 2018. His Peace has kept me since then and is continuing to do so. It is my hope and prayer, Beloved, that as you pray these prayers and meditate on the devotions, you will find His Peace to keep you as well.

In His Peace,
Brenda R. Cox

Contents

Word to the Reader

Holy Greetings Friend,

Prayer is how we *communicate* with God, and devotions enable us to *meditate* on His Word. PRAYERS & DEVOTIONS that Change Lives and Hearts will expand your prayer life, as well as empower you to receive more clarity while meditating on the Word of God.

As a Sunday School teacher for nearly 15 years, I have found that regardless of how long you have been walking with the Lord, or if you are new to the family of God, you will be strengthened, renewed, and able to find peace for your heart when you take your concerns to God in prayer.

This book will draw you closer to God while creating a more extraordinary prayer life and longing for Him. As you pray each prayer and read the devotions, there will be a desire to be still in His presence. God will speak to your heart as the prayers penetrate the atmosphere and the devotions speak life to your spirit. The readings will shut down the outside noise and distractions. And there, in His presence, you will find peace and rest for your soul.

I pray the Lord bless and keep you as you take this prayer journey and that you will see your life and the lives of those you pray for changed at Godspeed. And remember Philippians

4:6-7 says, "Be careful for nothing; but in everything by prayer and supplication with thanksgiving let your requests be made known unto God. And the peace of God, which passeth all understanding, shall keep your hearts and minds through Christ Jesus."

Now Beloved, silence the chatter and begin your prayer journey of peace as you go from faith to faith and glory to glory in Him.

In His Love,
Brenda R Cox

Morning Glory

Psalms 5:3
"My voice shalt thou hear in the morning, O LORD; in the morning will I direct my prayer unto thee and will look up."

Father, on this morning I come to You with a humble heart and mind, bowing down before Your throne, asking for forgiveness of my sins. I repent Father for every sin committed in thought word or deed. Create in me a clean heart, O God; and renewing a right spirit within me. Search me, O God, and know my heart: try me, and know my thoughts: and see if there be any wicked way in me and lead me in the way everlasting. Set a watch, O Lord, before my mouth; keep the door of my lips. For Your glory Lord, let the words of my mouth, and the meditation of my heart, be acceptable in thy sight, O Lord, my strength, and my redeemer as I praise and worship You. In Jesus' name, amen.

Scripture Reference

Psalm 141:3
Psalm 19:14
Psalm 51:10-19
Psalm 139:23-24

Thank You God for Jesus, the Holy Lamb of God who takes away the sins of the world. Thank You Savior for Your blood that washes me thoroughly from mine iniquity and cleanses me from my sin. I praise You Savior for Your resurrection that gives me a new life through the power of Holy Spirit. I invite You into my life on this morning as Master, Lord, and Savior and look unto You Jesus, as the author and finisher of my faith.

Holy Spirit of God, I invite You into my life today to lead, guide, and direct me as I go about my day. Spirit of God, order my steps in Thy word and let not any iniquity have dominion over me. In Jesus' name, amen.

Scripture Reference

Psalm 51:2
Psalm 119:133
John 1:29 b
Hebrews 12:2a

Heavenly Father, I come this morning to thank You for an abundantly blessed portion of life, health, and strength. I humble my heart and my mind before You today and ask for forgiveness of every sin committed in thought, word, or deed, known or unknown, in omission or commission. For Your name's sake Oh Lord, pardon me of my iniquities, transgressions, and trespasses as I forgive those who trespass against me.

I thank You Father for a new spirit and a heart of true repentance, for a heart of flesh that is tender toward You and Your way. Anything that is unlike You Father, take it away and replace it with the ways of eternal life in Christ Jesus. Let the words of my mouth and the meditations of my heart be acceptable in Your sight oh Lord. Keep guard over my mouth and watch over my lips so whatever I say is pleasing in Your sight and brings edification and builds up the hearers.

On today, Father, as I draw nigh to You and You to me, I bless Your name that my hands are clean, and my heart is purified. In Jesus' name, amen.

Scripture Reference

Matthew 6:12
Psalm 25:11
James 4:8
Ezekiel 36:26

In the name of Jesus Father, cause me to hear Thy lovingkindness in the morning for in Thee do I trust. Cause me to know the way wherein I should walk, as I lift up my soul unto thee. Teach me Your word, Father, for it is a lamp unto my feet and a light unto my path. Your Word reminds me that the Spirit of truth, is come, He will guide me into all truth: for He shall not speak of Himself; but whatsoever He shall hear, that shall He speak, and He will shew me things to come. Lead, guide, and direct me this day Father God in and through the Spirit of truth.

Father God, You said, "For I, saith the LORD, will be unto her a wall of fire round about, and will be the glory in the midst of her." As I go through this day, in the name of Jesus Father, be a wall of fire and a hedge of protection all around me, go before me make every crooked place straight. In Jesus' mighty name, amen.

Scripture Reference

Job 1:10
Psalm 143:8
Psalms 119:105
Zechariah 2:5
John 16:13

Arise and Go Up

Psalms 5:3
"My voice shalt thou hear in the morning,
O LORD; in the morning will I direct my
prayer unto thee and will look up."

In the morning when you arise, are you going to that sacred place of Bethel where you can communion with the Lord? Just as little children go to their parents' room first thing in the morning, God desires to hear us when we arise in the morning. We receive brand-new mercies every morning. This should be enough to send us running into His presence and direct our prayers unto Him for keeping us through the night.

Beloved, God would like nothing more for us to have powerful and divine encounters with Him in a sacred place every morning and see us erect *altars of remembrance*. However, we must be willing to *go up* to a place of worship in the spirit to receive all that He has to offer. And remember, God is a Spirit: and they that worship Him must worship Him in spirit and in truth. Therefore, how we worship is important as well.

Where is your Bethel, the place where you can arise and go up to first thing in the morning and anytime thereafter, to invoke the presence of the Lord? The place where you have built altars in remembrance of the distress God delivered you from by His Mighty Right Hand. Whether it be altars in your heart or something tangible, where is it? If you have it or when you find it, go to your Bethel again and again and receive the fellowship of God, just like Jacob did in Genesis 35:1. God said to Jacob, "arise and go to Bethel", the place where he encountered God.

Prayer

Father, in the name of Jesus, let it be my heart's desire to arise each morning and go to that special place where I can have an intimate encounter with You. In the name of Jesus, I pray Bethel remains in and with me during times of trouble as well as my times of joy, and that I never forget to erect an altar of remembrance for Your goodness and mercies You have bestowed upon my life. Amen.

Scripture References

Genesis 35:3
John 4:24

Body of Christ

1 Corinthians 12:26-27
"And whether one member suffer, all the members suffer with it; or one member be honoured, all the members rejoice with it. Now ye are the body of Christ, and members in particular."

Lord, I surrender my all to You on today and thank and praise You for the many blessings bestowed upon my life. I thank You for choosing me to be a part of the body of Christ and come on this day in the name of Jesus on behalf of the body of Christ.

Father, in the name of Jesus I pray that the body of Christ humble themselves and permit Jesus to be the head of the church. I thank You that Jesus is the beginning, the firstborn from the dead; and in all things He has the preeminence. Father thank You for putting all things under His feet and giving Him to be the head over all things to the church and the Body of Christ follows Him. All glory, honor, and praise to Jesus forever, amen.

Scripture Reference

Colossians 1:18
Ephesians 1:22
Galatians 3:27

Thank You, God, that the body of Christ follows Jesus like a lamb to the slaughter. Just as a sheep, before her shearers is dumb, so the body of Christ openeth not their mouth when given directions from God. I decree and declare that the Body of Christ are imitators of Christ.

Thank You Father for baptizing the body of Christ once again and they have put on the mind Christ Jesus and are filled with His thought's feelings and purposes. I decree and declare today, that the body of Christ walks in the Spirit of God and does not lust after the flesh. To God be the glory that the body of Christ has won the victory in and through Jesus. In Jesus' name, amen.

Scripture Reference

Galatians 5:16
Isaiah 53:7

Heavenly Father, I pray for the power of the Holy Spirit to reign over the body of Christ. I pray a mighty rushing wind and the purifying fire of the Holy Spirit rest, rule, reign, and abide on Your church. That the body of Christ, Your bride, be convicted of sin and be not conformed to this world: but be transformed by the renewing of their mind, that they may prove what is that good, and acceptable, and perfect, will of God.

Thank You, God, for Your supernatural power over the church to heal, perform miracles, and prophecy in Your name, for the glory of Kingdom. Lord I pray Thy kingdom come, Thy will be done in earth, as it is in heaven. That the grace of the Lord Jesus Christ, and the love of God, and the communion of the Holy Ghost, be within the body of Christ and the body of Christ reflects the Son of God. In Jesus' name, amen.

Scripture Reference

Matthew 6:10
2 Corinthians 13:14
Romans 12:2

Holy One of Israel, in the most powerful name above all names, the name of Jesus, I come on behalf of His bride, the church. God, You said, "If My people, which are called by My name, shall humble themselves, and pray, and seek My face, and turn from their wicked ways; then will I hear from heaven, and will forgive their sin, and will heal their land."

I pray on this day, that the body of Christ, with all lowliness and meekness, with longsuffering, forbearing one another in love and endeavouring to keep the unity of the Spirit in the bond of peace, would humble themselves, and pray, and seek Your face, and turn from their wicked ways. That they would be kind one to another, tenderhearted, forgiving one another, even as You God, for Christ's sake hath forgiven them. In Jesus' name, amen.

Scripture Reference

2 Chronicles 7:14
Ephesians 4:2-3
Ephesians 4:32

Ephesians 2: 19-22

Now, therefore, you are no longer strangers and foreigners, but fellow citizens with the saints and members of the household of God, having been built on the foundation of the apostles and prophets, Jesus Christ Himself being the chief cornerstone, in whom the whole building, being fitted together, grows into a holy temple in the Lord, in whom you also are being built together for a dwelling place of God in the Spirit.

If we are of the Spirit of God, why Beloved, are we still compromising and living like we belong to this world, and not to God? We are a part of the royal priesthood who is set apart from this world to do a mighty work for the glory of God. We possess a strong firm foundation given to us by those that were taught by Jesus Himself.

We are taught to love and pray for one another, to be there in times of trouble for one another, to even take one each other's burdens. It is the desire of God that we be joined together in the Spirit and become a holy temple, a place where He can come and dwell. This is *who WE are in CHRIST*.

It is time to rise and walk in the identity of who we are in the Body Christ Jesus. To become a dwelling place where the Spirit of God can enter in and engage in a time of holy intimacy with us. God is making a Kingdom call to all His children. He wants to take us to a higher place in Him. Will you answer the call to help take the Body of Christ to a higher place of praise in Him?

Prayer

Father God, in the most powerful name of Jesus, I pray that the eyes of the Body of Christ understanding be enlightened and that they may know what the hope of Your calling is, and the riches of the glory of Your inheritance in the saint. That the Body of Christ may know more clearly who they are in You. Help the Body of Christ I pray, to become a dwelling place for You and walk boldly in and with Your glory. I decree and declare the Body of Christ arise from their sleeping slumber and recognize You as King of the whole world and follow Your statues, decrees, and commands. That they would repent, walk in the Light of Christ and come out from among this world. I decree and declare that the Body of Christ become holy temples in the Lord and live as members of the household of God. In Jesus' name, amen.

Scripture Reference

Ephesians 1:18
Ephesians 2: 19-22

Marriage Harmony

Ephesians 5:21
Submit to one another out of reverence for Christ.

Unity

In the name of Jesus, I decree and declare the word of God over marriages that says, they twain shall be one flesh, so then they are no more twain, but one flesh. What therefore God hath joined together, let not man put asunder. I praise You Holy One that a threefold cord is not quickly broken.

In the name of Jesus of Nazareth, thank You God for drawing marriages nearer to You as they become one flesh through the unity and power of the Holy Spirit. Thank You Father for joining them fitly together and their bond is not easily broken. That spouses are continually submitting themselves one to another in the fear of God. Forbearing one another and forgiving one another in the love of Christ.

As spouses keep You Father, as the head of everything, bind them together in the love of Jesus Christ. Let them serve one another with a spirit of joy and a cheerful heart. I decree and declare greater communication and forgiveness, a greater love language, greater understanding, and greater intimacy. In the precious name of Jesus, amen.

Scripture Reference

Ephesians 5:21
Mark 10:8-9
Ecclesiastes 4:12
Colossians 3:13a

Husbands

In the name of Jesus, I decree and declare husbands love their wives, even as Christ also loved the church, and gave Himself for it. That husbands respond to their wives with tender love and kindness, and knowing a soft answer turneth away wrath, but grievous words stir up anger.

Praise be to God, for husbands are faithful, true, and honest to their wives, and dwell with them according to knowledge, giving honor unto the wife, as unto the weaker vessel, and as being heirs together of the grace of life, that their prayers be not hindered.

Thank You, God, that husbands love their wives as they love themselves. In Jesus' name, amen.

Scripture References

Ephesians 5:25; 28
Proverbs 15:1
1 Peter 3:7

Wife

Heavenly Father, Your word tells us that whoso findeth a wife findeth a good thing, and obtaineth favour of the LORD. I thank You God that I am a good thing to my husband, and he has obtained favor with You and all those around him. That my husband's heart doth safely trust in me, so that he shall have no need of spoil. I will do him good and not evil all the days of my life.

I bless You Lord, that I am a prudent wife, a virtuous woman, and a crown to my husband. I submit myself unto my own husbands, as unto the Lord. For the husband is the head of the wife, even as Christ is the head of the church: and He is the Saviour of the body. I decree and declare my husband is the head over my life as Jesus is to the church. Therefore, as the church is subject unto Christ, so let me be to my own husband in everything. In Jesus' name, amen.

Scripture Reference

Ephesians 5:22-24
Proverbs 12:4a
Proverbs 19:14b
Proverbs 31:11-12

Godly Submission

Ephesians 5:21
Submit to one another out of reverence for Christ.

When we love and trust God, obeying Him is not burdensome as it becomes our hearts desire to please Him. This also includes submitting to one another.

Submitting can sometimes seem to be an extremely offensive word in marriages if we look at it from the world's perspective. In the world, this could mean that you are weak or have surrendered yourself over to the demands of a tyrant. But when there is a *Godly submission*, a sweet surrender takes place.

When a husband and wife submit to one another out of reverence for Christ, each of them with a cheerful heart takes on the act of servanthood. This is where the sweetness of surrender comes in, as every act performed is unto the Lord. While spouses grow more focused on God and a desire develops to please God, peace that passes all understanding enters the atmosphere. With this peace comes the presence of God, and His glory consumes the union with a continuous state of joy and harmony.

Prayer

Father God, thank You for the peace that comes from submitting to You and the atmosphere it creates in marriages. I thank You that I and my husband/wife enjoy the fruits of sweet surrender to You and now and forevermore. In Jesus' name, amen.

Scripture References

Ephesians 5:21
Philippians 4:7a

Blessings for Our Children

Proverbs 22:6
"Train up a child in the way he should go: and when he is old, he will not depart from it."

Thank You Lord God for children, they are a blessing and a gift from You. Trust, faith, purity, and joy fill their hearts. Help me to be more like children when I come before Your throne, full of *trust and faith*. In the name of Jesus, I come to Your throne God, full of trust and childlike faith, praying for children. My children, nieces, nephews, grandchildren, children in my community, city, and state, in this country, and around the globe. As I usher them into Your presence I thank You, Holy One of Israel for keeping them safe as they take refuge in You. For hiding them in the shadow of Your wings. I thank You that Your rod and staff comfort them during their times of trouble, and You are their hiding place, and they are preserved from trouble. That You are their lamplight, a lamp unto their feet and a light unto their path, and they are not led into temptation but are delivered from evil. In Jesus' name, amen.

Scripture References

Psalm 17:8
Psalm 23:4
Psalm 32:7
Psalms 119:105

In the name of Jesus, I pray for the power and peace of the Holy Spirit of God to fall upon children around the globe today. That Your glory God would surround them like a wall of fire and a hedge of protection. I bless the name of the Lord that He has saved them from the hand of him that hated them and redeemed them from the hand of the enemy. I bind every corruptible relationship that has been sent by the enemy to the children in the name of Jesus.

I loose upon the children the Spirit of Truth, the Spirit of the living God, the mind of Christ, the fruits of the spirit, the wisdom, knowledge and understanding, and the fear of the Lord. I decree and declare my children will grow up to be the head and not the tail, they shalt be above only, and shalt not be beneath. Blessed shalt they be when they come in, and blessed shalt they be when thou go out. I decree and declare they walk in the righteousness of the Lord and serve Him now and forevermore, in Jesus' name, amen.

Scripture References

Psalm 32:7
Matthew 6:13
Deuteronomy 28:6;13

Father God, it is in the name of Jesus I pray for the children today. That You Lord bless and keep them and make Your face shine on them and be gracious to them; that You turn Your face toward them and give them peace. Father, I pray that their steps be ordered in Your word.

I decree and declare that they walk after You, fear You, keep Your commandments, obey Your voice, and hold fast to You. I thank You Holy God that my children hear Your voice, and serve You and You alone.

I decree and declare that my children walk before You faithfully, with integrity of heart and uprightness, according to Your word Father. That they do everything according to all that Your word has commanded.

I thank You Holy God that they have a heart and mind to follow You and learn to obey the decrees, precepts, and commands You have given. It is in the Almighty name of Jesus I pray, amen.

Scripture Reference

Numbers 6:24-26
Deuteronomy 13:4
1 Kings 9:4

College Students

On today, it is in the name of above all names, the name of Jesus, that I pray for children, here and around the globe. Especially for those who are away at college or have joined the military. There can at times be so much pressure on these children, like they must prove to others that they have finally reached adulthood. During these times, bad choices can be made, especially if children are deceived by the enemy. But Your word declares that the fear of the LORD is the beginning of wisdom, and knowledge of the Holy One is understanding.

I thank You Father that these children fear You and have wisdom, knowledge, and understanding in abundance and they share it with others. That they can declare to others Oh taste and see that the LORD is good, how blessed is the man who takes refuge in Him. That they are strong and courageous. For Your word says, "do not be afraid; do not be discouraged, for the LORD your God will be with you wherever you go." Thank You Father that the children know that You are with them, and they trust in You with all their heart and lean not on their own understanding; in all their ways submit to You Lord, and You will make their paths straight.

I thank Father God, that their hearts cry to You is "show me Your ways, LORD, teach me Your paths. Guide me in Your truth and teach me, for You are God my Savior, and my hope is in You all day long." In the most powerful name of Jesus, amen.

Scripture Reference

Proverbs 9:10
Psalm 34:8
Joshua 1:9
Proverbs 3:5-6

Children Taught of the Lord

Proverbs 22:6
"Train up a child in the way he should go: and
when he is old, he will not depart from it."

Children are a gift from the Lord and should be treated as such, not as a burden. They are a heritage from the Lord and are given over to their parents, who are charged to bring them up in the nurture and admonition of the Lord. As parents or whoever has guardianship over children, raising them up in the way of the Lord is of the utmost.

Let us train up our precious children in godliness. Teaching them the ways of God, and to love Him with all the heart. By doing this we know, according to the word of God, when they are old they will not depart from it.

Prayer

In the name of Jesus, thank You, Father, that we can decree and declare over our children what Paul said to Timothy in 2 Timothy 3:15 "that from a child thou hast known the holy scriptures, which are able to make thee wise unto salvation through faith which is in Christ Jesus." In Jesus' name, amen.

Scripture References

Psalm 127:3-5
2 Timothy 3:15
Proverbs 22:6
Deuteronomy 6:5-9
Ephesians 6:4

Restoration and Healing

1 Peter 2:24
"Who His own self bare our sins in His own body on the tree, that we, being dead to sins, should live unto righteousness: by whose stripes ye were healed."

Father, in the name of Jesus I thank You for the blood of Jesus that heals and washes away all sin. I pray for the healing power of the blood of Jesus to touch all those that have sickness in their bodies. I decree and declare Your word that says Jesus was wounded for our transgressions, He was bruised for our iniquities: the chastisement of our peace was upon Him; and with His stripes we are healed. I decree and declare this word over myself and those that are stricken with disease. There is Balm in Gilead, and His name is Jesus. I apply the Balm of Gilead from the crown of their heads to the souls of their feet that they may rise and be healed in the healing name of Jesus and pick up their beds and walk. I thank You Father for Your healing virtue and am reminded that You are the Lord who heals, and You are healing them at this very moment. In Jesus' name, Amen.

Scripture Reference

Isaiah 53:5
Isaiah 1:6
Exodus 15:26
John 1:29

Blessed Savior, I magnify and glorify Your Holy name and thank You that You are the God who heals all our souls' diseases. That You heal the brokenhearted and bind up their wounds. And the prayer of faith shall save the sick, and You shall raise them up; and if he has committed sins, they shall be forgiven him.

I decree and declare Your word that says behold, I will bring it health and cure, and I will cure them. Thank You heavenly Father for curing all those who are sick and stricken with disease. For being the God Who forgives all our iniquities and Who heals all our diseases: Who redeems our life from destruction and who crowns us with lovingkindness and tender mercies every morning.

You are the God who heals and restores. It is in the name of Jesus, and through the Spirit of the living God that I send this word out to heal and deliver from destruction, amen.

Scripture Reference

Jeremiah 33:6
Psalm 103:3-4
James 5:15

Great is the Lord, and greatly to be praised. Father, In the name of Jesus, I come in accord with the Saints of God, to lift up Your holy righteous name. I believe Your promises are yes and amen and stand firm on them as I usher_____ into Your presence for healing. I know that You are the God Who heals and gives power to the weak and to those who have not might, You increase their strength. I decree and declare in the name of Jesus, that _____ strength shall be renewed, he/she shall mount up with wings like eagles, he/she shall run and not be weary, he/she shall walk and not fall. For You Lord are good and Your mercy is everlasting. I decree and declare this prayer in the name of Jesus, amen.

Scripture Reference

2 Corinthians 1:20
Psalm 145:3
Isaiah 40:29;31
Exodus 15:26
Psalm 100:5

God Our Healer

Luke 17:11-19
11 Now it happened as He went to Jerusalem that He passed through the midst of Samaria and Galilee. 12 Then as He entered a certain village, there met Him ten men who were lepers, who stood afar off. 13 And they lifted up their voices and said, "Jesus, Master, have mercy on us!" 14 So when He saw them, He said to them, "Go, show yourselves to the priests." And so it was that as they went, they were cleansed. 15 And one of them, when he saw that he was healed, returned, and with a loud voice glorified God, 16 and fell down on his face at His feet, giving Him thanks. And he was a Samaritan.

Today let us not forget all of what we have been healed and delivered from. When you look back and see all of what God has carried you through, not to mention those things you were unaware of, surely you are grateful! I can't help but praise Him, just like the leper did after he had been healed from leprosy. He went back to Jesus, fell at His feet, and began to thank Him.

If we go back a few days, weeks, months, or years, we could gather up a praise for our healing that would send the enemy fleeing for his life! More than that, let us thank God for someone else's healing and deliverance to cripple that lying wonder. Let us cripple the devil today with our praise, worship, and thanksgiving to God our Healer!

Prayer

Thank You Father God for being the LORD that heals! It is with our praise we can fight the battle before us without knowing it is even there. Thank You for a mouth that continually sings Your praises. In Jesus Name, amen.

Scripture References

Luke 17:11-19
Exodus 15:26b

Overcoming Thought Life

Romans 12:2
"And be not conformed to this world: but be ye transformed by the renewing of your mind, that ye may prove what is that good, and acceptable, and perfect, will of God."

In the name of Jesus, I decree and declare all power and take authority over my thought life. Father God, Your word says be not conformed to this world: but be ye transformed by the renewing of your mind, that ye may prove what is that good, and acceptable, and perfect, will of God. Today, I renew my mind in the name of Jesus and set my affection on things above, not on things on the earth. I gird up the loins of my mind, and am sober, and hope to the end for the grace that is to be brought unto me at the revelation of Jesus Christ.

For I know that as I walk in the flesh, I do not war after the flesh, for the weapons of my warfare are not carnal, but mighty through God to the pulling down of strong holds. In the power and authority of Jesus of Nazareth, I cast down imaginations, every high thing that exalteth itself against the knowledge of God and bring into captivity every thought to the obedience of Christ.

This is the day which the LORD hath made; I will rejoice and be glad in it. I will trust in the LORD with all my heart; and lean not unto my own understanding. In all my ways I will acknowledge Him, and He shall direct my paths. I bless You, Lord, for Your word is a lamp unto my feet and a light unto my path. In Jesus' name, amen.

Scripture Reference

Romans 12:2
1 Peter 1:13
Colossians 3:2
2 Corinthians 10:3-5
Psalms 118:24
Psalms 119:105
Proverbs 3:5-6

Father God, I thank You that I have the mind of Christ. And since I have the mind of Christ, on this day, I decree and declare that I will not be conformed to this world: but be transformed by the renewing of my mind, that I may prove what is that good, and acceptable, and perfect, will of God. Whatsoever things are true, whatsoever things are honest, whatsoever things are just, whatsoever things are pure, whatsoever things are lovely, whatsoever things are of good report; if there be any virtue, and if there be any praise, I will think on these things. In Jesus' mighty name, amen.

Scripture Reference

Romans 12:2
Philippians 2:5 a
Philippians 4:8

Today I cast down imaginations and every high thing that exalteth itself against the knowledge of God and bringing into captivity every thought to the obedience of Christ. I am casting all my cares upon Him; for He careth for me.

God, You hath not given us the spirit of fear, but of power, and of love, and of a sound mind. I thank You, Lord, for a sound mind and declare Thou wilt keep me in perfect peace, as my mind is stayed on Thee: because I trusteth in Thee. I trust in You Lord and thank You for peace of mind today and every day. I will be sober and vigilant; because my adversary the devil, as a roaring lion, walketh about, seeking whom he may devour. I decree and declare that the peace of God, which passeth all understanding, shall keep my heart and mind through Christ Jesus. In Jesus' name, amen.

Scripture References

2 Timothy 1:7
Isaiah 26:3
2 Corinthians 10:5
1 Peter 5:7-8
Philippians 4:7

Winning The Battle of Your Mind

Ephesians 4:23
And be renewed in the spirit of your mind And
that ye put on the new man, which after God is
created in righteousness and true holiness

To be renewed in the spirit of the mind, a transformation must take place. The bible tells us to be not conformed to this world: but be ye *transformed* by the renewing of your mind, that ye may prove what is that good, and acceptable, and perfect, will of God. Transformation starts by releasing the past and allowing Holy Spirit to come in and purge your heart and mind, and uproot every ungodly thought, act, and scene, and replacing those with the mind of Christ.

God does not want us to be held hostage by the thoughts that plague our minds. He does not want us to become paralyzed in fear by lies from the enemy. Regardless of the situation and circumstances that will arise and the inner idle chatter Beloved, He wants you and me to press in and keep trusting Him. His desire is for us to be established in a new transformed mind and stand on His Word. To move forward in His righteousness and true holiness and bring Him glory due to His name.

Prayer

Heavenly Father, on today I give my heart to You once again. I receive the infilling of Your Holy Spirit and am renewed in the spirit of my mind to win every battle the enemy sends in in my atmosphere. In Jesus' name, amen.

Scripture References

Romans 12:2
Ephesians 4:23
1 Corinthians 2:16

Spirit of Heaviness

James 4:7
Submit yourselves therefore to God. Resist
the devil, and he will flee from you.

In the name of Jesus, I bind the spirit of heaviness that has come upon _____ and those voices that have become louder in his/her ears and minds telling him/her that suicide is the only way out of a situation. I decree and declare that when the enemy shall come in like a flood, the Spirit of the Lord shall lift up a standard against him in his/her life. That as _____ submits himself/herself before God and resist the devil, the devil will flee from their presence. I praise Your name, Father God, that You will heal their broken heart bind up their wounds and they live life more abundantly.

On this day, I loose upon _____, the spirit of comfort, the garment of praise, and the oil of joy. I decree and declare _____ is tree of righteousness planted by the Lord God Almighty and _____ life will surely glorify our Father in heaven. In that matchless name of Jesus', I pray this prayer, amen.

Scripture References

Isaiah 59:19
Isaiah 61:3
Psalm 147:3
Isaiah 61:3
James 4:7

I pray in the name of Jesus, that _____ joy is restored, and that he/she has peace that passes all understanding. That _____ believes the word of God that says, "the LORD thy God will hold thy right hand, saying unto thee, fear not; I will help thee." That the God of hope fill him/her with all joy and peace in believing, that he/she may abound in hope, through the power of the Holy Ghost.

In the mighty name of Jesus, I pray that the Lord our God gives _____ beauty for ashes, the oil of joy for mourning, and the garment of praise for the spirit of heaviness.

That Your glory God would break forth in _____ life and their days be lighter and their nights be brighter. That they are restored the joy of their salvation and walk in the light of Christ Jesus now and forevermore. In Jesus' name amen.

Scripture References

Isaiah 41:13
Romans 15:13
Philippians 4:7

Father, Your word declares that a merry heart maketh a cheerful countenance: but by sorrow of the heart, the spirit is broken. I pray in the name of Jesus for _____, that he/she has a cheerful countenance, no matter what circumstances arise.

Your word says that the blessing of the LORD, it maketh rich, and He added no sorrow with it. I decree and declare in the name of Jesus that _____ has the blessings of the Lord upon his/her life and sorrow is evicted.

I declare that the rod and staff of the Lord our God comfort _____ and bring him/her peace that passes all understanding. That the righteousness of the Lord goes before him/her, and His glory be his/her rearguard. In Jesus' matchless name, amen.

Scripture References

Proverbs 10:22
Proverbs 15:13
Psalm 23:4b
Isaiah 58:8b
Philippians 4:7

Remove the Spirit of Witchcraft

Leviticus 19:31
Regard not them that have familiar spirits,
neither seek after wizards, to be defiled
by them: I am the LORD your God.

Lord Your word declares "Thou shalt not suffer a witch to live." On today I plead the blood of Jesus and bind and rebuke the princes and powers in the air and command them to go in the name of Jesus. The hand of the Lord be against all witches and warlocks at all satanic altars and high places, and they come to an immediate end, in the name of Jesus.

I decree and declare the fire of God to fall on all idols, rituals, and sacrifices in this land. That they be as chaff which the winds drive away with the angels of the Lord chasing them on. In the name of Jesus, I claim this country for God, and plead the blood of Jesus in the north, south, east, and the west. I bind and break every lying chain and all covenants made between God's creation and the prince of this air, in the name of Jesus.

I pray for and loose the power of the Holy Spirit of God and I decree and declare the Spirit of Truth to fall upon this nation today. I pray and declare the glory of God be a blanket over the United States of America and be a wall of fire and a hedge of protection against every rudiment of evil the devil and his agents attempt to pour out.

For Your glory Lord, I pray and declare Your presence, dominion, authority, and blessings be known to all in the United States of America and around the globe. In Jesus' name, amen

Scripture Reference

Exodus 22:18
Psalms 1:4

Father, Your Word declares to "Let no one be found among you who sacrifices their son or daughter in the fire, who practices divination or sorcery, interprets omens, engages in witchcraft, or casts spells, or who is a medium or spiritist or who consults the dead. Anyone who does these things is detestable to the Lord." On today, in the name above every name, that matchless name of Jesus, I come. In all power and authority that has been given to me through the shedding of the blood of Jesus, I come. As David came against Goliath, I come against those who sacrifice their son or daughter in the fire, who practices divination or sorcery, interprets omens: who engages in witchcraft, or casts spells, or who is a medium or spiritist or who consults the dead.

I pray for those who practice such things and ask Father that the eyes of their understanding be enlightened, and they know what is the hope of Your calling, and what the riches of the glory of Your inheritance in the saints. That the eyes of their hearts and the doors of their understanding be illuminated. That they would come out of the dark and walk in the marvelous light of Jesus Christ and accept Him as their Lord and Savior.

In the power and authority of Christ Jesus, I come and break the control, force, and influence of all witchcraft, spells, curses, medium and spiritist. I decree and declare that it cannot prosper against me and my family in the name of Jesus. I cancel and destroy every rudiment of evil, every assignment, every attack of the enemy, every curse or negative word ever spoken over our lives and render them useless in the most powerful name of Jesus Christ. God, You are awesome, powerful, and mighty to save and I declare that we have victory in and through the blood of Jesus, amen.

Scripture Reference

Deuteronomy 18:10-12
Ephesians 1:18

Be Not Defiled

Leviticus 19:31
Regard not them that have familiar spirits,
neither seek after wizards, to be defiled
by them: I am the LORD your God.

There are so many different spirits people are operating in and, now more than ever we must be mindful of *who* we are associating with, and the *type of spirit* they operate in. We must use our ***Godly spiritual discernment***, to ensure we do not get entangled with or bewitched by such individuals.

God is the great I AM. He is Jehovah Jireh, our Provider, and desires for us to look to ***Him*** for everything we need, including insight or wisdom. The bible reminds us that if there is anyone who lacks wisdom, let him ask of God, that giveth to all men liberally, and upbraideth not; and it shall be given him. When asking and trusting God who is our source of all wisdom, there is no need to seek spirits and wizard who cannot comprehend the ways or the mind of God who created this universe. Therefore, let us separate ourselves from these spirits that creep around in high and dark places and be not defiled. Let us purpose ourselves to live a holy life that is pleasing to God, so He does not set His face against our soul.

Prayer

Holy God, I thank You for spiritual wisdom, guidance, and discernment in all that I do. In the name of Jesus, permit me to see the spirits that I am associating with and separate from those which are not of You. Your word declares that we wrestle not against flesh and blood, but against principalities, against powers, against the rulers of the darkness of this world, against spiritual wickedness in high places. I thank You, Father, for granting me Your favor, so I do not get ensnared with spiritual wickedness in high places of any sort. In Jesus' most excellent name, amen.

Scripture References

Leviticus 19:31
Leviticus 20:6
Ephesians 6:12
James 1:5

Government
Armed Forces
First Responders

Government

Lord, You have a kingdom purpose during these dangerous times in this country. You sit high and look low and are not surprised by anything that is going on. You are Alpha and Omega, the beginning and the end, and the Almighty God in between. You know what this country is about to deal with. We ask today, in the name of Jesus, that You lead guide, and direct the leaders of this country.

Your word declares "For God is the King of all the earth." King of all the Earth, I call upon You now and pray for our president and their cabinet, as well as the vice president and their advisors. I pray that they would seek godly wisdom before making any decisions. That they would be Spirit-led in their decision making on how to lead this country. That they would humble themselves in Your sight. I pray they have an ear to hear You speak to them daily while facing the many issues concerning this nation. I pray for godly guidance, wisdom, knowledge, and understanding, as it is for lack of guidance a nation falls, but victory is won through many advisers.

I pray for those who create laws and bills. That they would work together peacefully and create laws to enable us to live peaceful and quiet lives in all godliness and holiness.

Your word reminds us that every kingdom divided against itself will be ruined, and every city or household divided against itself will not stand. In the name of Jesus, I come against the division in this county, especially between our government officials. I praise God, that they work together in peace and harmony. That all parties and people lay down their agenda and pick up their assignment from our heavenly Father and work together for the advancement of this country.

You told us in the bible that "If my people, which are called by my name, shall humble themselves, and pray, and seek my face, and turn from their wicked ways; then will I hear from heaven, and will forgive their sin, and will heal their land." I praise You, God, that those who work for this government have become humbled, and they pray daily. That they are praying and seeking Your face for every tiny matter and turning from all forms of wickedness. In Jesus' name, amen.

Scripture References

2 Chronicles 7:14
Proverbs 11:14
Psalm 47:7a
1 Timothy 2:1-2
Matthew 12:15
James 4:10

Armed Forces

I thank You, God, for the mighty men and women of valor who fight for our freedoms here in the United States of America every day. For being the God who teacheth their hands to war, and their fingers to fight. I decree and declare that before going into battle, divine protection is with them. You declared to David, "Sit thou at my right hand, until I make thine enemies thy footstool." I decree and declare that their enemies are their footstool.

When they are under pressure, I thank You Mighty God, for giving them divine strategies as You gave to Joshua when fighting the battle of Jericho. Just as you allowed Shadrach, Meshach, and Abednego victory while going through and coming out of the fiery furnace, I thank You for allowing these men and women of valor to walk in and out of battle with victory in Jesus.

As these men and women stand in the gap and protect this country, I pray that the Captain of the Host of the Lord be in their defense, in Jesus' name, amen.

Scripture Reference

Joshua 5:14
Psalms 144:1

Healthcare Workers and Paramedics

Our Healthcare Workers and Paramedics who work so tirelessly to meet the emergency needs of the citizens of this country; we thank You for them, God. I pray for their peace of mind and strength for their bodies, that it never fail. That they will continue to rejoice while on duty and You Lord preserve their going out and their coming in from this time forth, and even for evermore.

They are working longer hours with less help and now more than ever before, in some locations, being frowned upon. But God, I thank You, for granting them a heart of compassion to become lifesavers and caretakers for those who are unable to care for themselves. I thank You Father, for enabling them to be peacemakers and a comfort to family members when they are scared and alone. I pray in the name of Jesus, for walls of fire and hedges of protection to be erected all around about them, and Your angels keep charge over them. Let them know Father, as they passest through the waters, You will be with them; and through the rivers, they shall not overflow them: when they walkest through the fire, they shalt not be burned; neither shall the flame kindle upon them.

Father God, it is in the precious powerful name of Jesus I pray that the Healthcare Workers and Paramedics do not be weary in well doing: for in due season they shall reap, if they faint not. In Jesus' name, amen.

Scripture References

Psalms 121:8
Isaiah 43:2
Galatians 6:9

Scripture
References

Genesis 35:3

> And let us arise and go up to Bethel; and I will make there an altar unto God, who answered me in the day of my distress, and was with me in the way which I went.

Exodus 15:26

> And said, if thou wilt diligently hearken to the voice of the LORD thy God, and wilt do that which is right in his sight, and wilt give ear to his commandments, and keep all his statutes, I will put none of these diseases upon thee, which I have brought upon the Egyptians: for I am the LORD that healeth thee.

Exodus 22:18

> Thou shalt not suffer a witch to live.

Leviticus 19:31

> Regard not them that have familiar spirits, neither seek after wizards, to be defiled by them: I am the LORD your God.

Leviticus 20:6 -7

> And the soul that turneth after such as have familiar spirits, and after wizards, to go a whoring after them, I will even set my face against that soul, and will cut him off from among his people. Sanctify yourselves therefore, and be ye holy: for I am the LORD your God.

Numbers 6:24-26

The LORD bless thee and keep thee: The LORD make his face shine upon thee, and be gracious unto thee: The LORD lift up his countenance upon thee, and give thee peace. 27And they shall put my name upon the children of Israel; and I will bless them.

Deuteronomy 6:5-9

And thou shalt love the LORD thy God with all thine heart, and with all thy soul, and with all thy might. And these words, which I command thee this day, shall be in thine heart: And thou shalt teach them diligently unto thy children, and shalt talk of them when thou sittest in thine house, and when thou walkest by the way, and when thou liest down, and when thou risest up. And thou shalt bind them for a sign upon thine hand, and they shall be as frontlets between thine eyes. And thou shalt write them upon the posts of thy house, and on thy gates.

Deuteronomy 13:4

Ye shall walk after the LORD your God, and fear him, and keep his commandments, and obey his voice, and ye shall serve him, and cleave unto him.

Deuteronomy 18:10

There shall not be found among you anyone that maketh his son or his daughter to pass through the fire, or that useth divination, or an observer of times, or an enchanter, or a witch, Or a charmer, or a consulter with familiar spirits, or a wizard, or a necromancer. For all that do these things are an abomination unto the LORD: and because of these abominations the LORD thy God doth drive them out from before thee.

Deuteronomy 28:6

Blessed shalt thou be when thou comest in, and blessed shalt thou be when thou goest out.

Deuteronomy 28:13

And the LORD shall make thee the head, and not the tail; and thou shalt be above only, and thou shalt not be beneath; if that thou hearken unto the commandments of the LORD thy God, which I command thee this day, to observe and to do them.

Joshua 1:9

Have not I commanded thee? Be strong and of a good courage; be not afraid, neither be thou dismayed: for the LORD thy God is with thee whithersoever thou goest.

Deuteronomy 31:6

Be strong and of a good courage, fear not, nor be afraid of them: for the LORD thy God, he it is that doth go with thee; he will not fail thee, nor forsake thee.

Joshua 5:14a

> And he said, Nay; but as captain of the host of the LORD am I now come. And Joshua fell on his face to the earth, and did worship, and said unto him, What saith my lord unto his servant?

1 Kings 9:4

> And if thou wilt walk before me, as David thy father walked, in integrity of heart, and in uprightness, to do according to all that I have commanded thee, and wilt keep my statutes and my judgments.

1 Kings 17:13

> And Elijah said unto her, Fear not; go and do as thou hast said: but make me thereof a little cake first, and bring it unto me, and after make for thee and for thy son.

2 Chronicles 7:14

> If my people, which are called by my name, shall humble themselves, and pray, and seek my face, and turn from their wicked ways; then will I hear from heaven, and will forgive their sin, and will heal their land.

Job 1:10

> Hast not thou made an hedge about him, and about his house, and about all that he hath on every side? thou hast blessed the work of his hands, and his substance is increased in the land.

Psalms 1:4

> The ungodly are not so: but are like the chaff which the wind driveth away.

Psalms 5:3

> My voice shalt thou hear in the morning, O LORD; in the morning will I direct my prayer unto thee and will look up.

Psalms 16:1

> Preserve me, O God: for in thee do I put my trust.

Psalms 17:8

> Keep me as the apple of the eye, hide me under the shadow of thy wings.

Psalm 19:14

> Let the words of my mouth, and the meditation of my heart, be acceptable in thy sight, O LORD, my strength, and my redeemer.

Psalms 23:4

> Yea, though I walk through the valley of the shadow of death, I will fear no evil: for thou art with me; thy rod and thy staff they comfort me.

Psalm 25:11

> For thy name's sake, O LORD, pardon mine iniquity; for it is great.

Psalms 30:2

> O LORD my God, I cried unto thee, and thou hast healed me.

Psalms 32:7

> Thou art my hiding place; thou shalt preserve me from trouble; thou shalt compass me about with songs of deliverance. Selah.

Psalms 34:8

> O taste and see that the LORD is good: blessed is the man that trusteth in him.

Psalm 51:2

> Wash me throughly from mine iniquity, and cleanse me from my sin.

Psalm 51:10-19

> Create in me a clean heart, O God; and renew a right spirit within me. 11Cast me not away from thy presence; and take not thy holy spirit from me. 12Restore unto me the joy of thy salvation; and uphold me with thy free spirit. 13Then will I teach transgressors thy ways; and sinners shall be converted unto thee. Deliver me

from bloodguiltiness, O God, thou God of my salvation: and my tongue shall sing aloud of thy righteousness. 15O Lord, open thou my lips; and my mouth shall shew forth thy praise. 16For thou desirest not sacrifice; else would I give it: thou delightest not in burnt offering. 17The sacrifices of God are a broken spirit: a broken and a contrite heart, O God, thou wilt not despise. 18Do good in thy good pleasure unto Zion: build thou the walls of Jerusalem. 19Then shalt thou be pleased with the sacrifices of righteousness, with burnt offering and whole burnt offering: then shall they offer bullocks upon thine altar.

Psalms 100:5

For the LORD is good; his mercy is everlasting; and his truth endureth to all generations.

Psalm 103:3-4

Who forgiveth all thine iniquities; who healeth all thy diseases; Who redeemeth thy life from destruction; who crowneth thee with lovingkindness and tender mercies.

Psalms 106:10

And he saved them from the hand of him that hated them, and redeemed them from the hand of the enemy.

Psalm 110:1

The LORD said unto my Lord, Sit thou at my right hand, until I make thine enemies thy footstool.

Psalms 113:9

He maketh the barren woman to keep house, and to be a joyful mother of children. Praise ye the LORD.

Psalms 118:24

This is the day which the LORD hath made; we will rejoice and be glad in it.

Psalm 119:15

I will meditate in thy precepts and have respect unto thy ways.

Psalms 119:105

Thy word is a lamp unto my feet, and a light unto my path.

Psalm 119:133

Order my steps in thy word: and let not any iniquity have dominion over me.

Psalms 121:8

The LORD shall preserve thy going out and thy coming in from this time forth, and even for evermore.

Psalm 127:3-5

Lo, children are an heritage of the LORD: and the fruit of the womb is his reward. As arrows are in the hand of a mighty man; so are children of the youth. Happy is the man that hath his quiver full of them: they shall not be ashamed, but they shall speak with the enemies in the gate.

Psalm 139:23-24

Search me, O God, and know my heart: try me, and know my thoughts: And see if there be any wicked way in me, and lead me in the way everlasting.

Psalm 141:3

Set a watch, O LORD, before my mouth; keep the door of my lips.

Psalm 143:8

Cause me to hear thy lovingkindness in the morning; for in thee do I trust: cause me to know the way wherein I should walk; for I lift up my soul unto thee.

Psalms 144:1

Blessed be the LORD my strength, which teacheth my hands to war, and my fingers to fight.

Psalms 145:3

Great is the LORD, and greatly to be praised; and his greatness is unsearchable.

Psalms 147:3

He healeth the broken in heart, and bindeth up their wounds.

Proverbs 3:5-6

Trust in the LORD with all thine heart; and lean not unto thine own understanding. In all thy ways acknowledge him, and he shall direct thy paths.

Proverbs 9:10

The fear of the LORD is the beginning of wisdom: and the knowledge of the holy is understanding.

Proverbs 10:22

The blessing of the LORD, it maketh rich, and he addeth no sorrow with it.

Proverbs 12:4a

A virtuous woman is a crown to her husband: but she that maketh ashamed is as rottenness in his bones.

Proverbs 15:1

A soft answer turneth away wrath: but grievous words stir up anger.

Proverbs 15:13

> A merry heart maketh a cheerful countenance: but by sorrow of the heart the spirit is broken.

Proverbs 19:14b

> House and riches are the inheritance of fathers: and a prudent wife is from the LORD.

Proverbs 22:6

> Train up a child in the way he should go: and when he is old, he will not depart from it.

Proverbs 31:11-12

> The heart of her husband doth safely trust in her, so that he shall have no need of spoil. She will do him good and not evil all the days of her life.

Ecclesiastes 4:12

> And if one prevail against him, two shall withstand him; and a threefold cord is not quickly broken.

Isaiah 1:6

> From the sole of the foot even unto the head there is no soundness in it; but wounds, and bruises, and putrifying sores: they have not been closed, neither bound up, neither mollified with ointment.

Isaiah 26:3

> Thou wilt keep him in perfect peace, whose mind is stayed on thee: because he trusteth in thee.

Isaiah 40:4

> Every valley shall be exalted, and every mountain and hill shall be made low: and the crooked shall be made straight, and the rough places plain.

Isaiah 40:31

> But they that wait upon the LORD shall renew their strength; they shall mount up with wings as eagles; they shall run, and not be weary; and they shall walk, and not faint.

Isaiah 41:10

> Fear thou not; for I am with thee: be not dismayed; for I am thy God: I will strengthen thee; yea, I will help thee; yea, I will uphold thee with the right hand of my righteousness.

Isaiah 41:13

> For I the LORD thy God will hold thy right hand, saying unto thee, Fear not; I will help thee.

Isaiah 43:2

> When thou passest through the waters, I will be with thee; and through the rivers, they shall not overflow thee: when thou walkest through the fire, thou shalt not be burned; neither shall the flame kindle upon thee.

Isaiah 53:5

> But he was wounded for our transgressions, he was bruised for our iniquities: the chastisement of our peace was upon him; and with his stripes we are healed.

Isaiah 53:7

> He was oppressed, and he was afflicted, yet he opened not his mouth: he is brought as a lamb to the slaughter, and as a sheep before her shearers is dumb, so he openeth not his mouth.

Isaiah 54:13

> And all thy children shall be taught of the LORD; and great shall be the peace of thy children.

Isaiah 58:8

> Then shall thy light break forth as the morning, and thine health shall spring forth speedily: and thy righteousness shall go before thee; the glory of the LORD shall be thy rereward.

Isaiah 59:19

> So shall they fear the name of the LORD from the west, and his glory from the rising of the sun. When the enemy shall come in like a flood, the Spirit of the LORD shall lift up a standard against him.

Isaiah 61:3

> To appoint unto them that mourn in Zion, to give unto them beauty for ashes, the oil of joy for mourning, the garment of praise for the spirit of heaviness; that they might be called trees of righteousness, the planting of the LORD, that he might be glorified.

Isaiah 61:7

> For your shame ye shall have double; and for confusion they shall rejoice in their portion: therefore in their land they shall possess the double: everlasting joy shall be unto them.

Jeremiah 17:14

> Heal me, O LORD, and I shall be healed; save me, and I shall be saved: for thou art my praise.

Jeremiah 29:11

> For I know the thoughts that I think toward you, saith the LORD, thoughts of peace, and not of evil, to give you an expected end.

Jeremiah 30:17

> For I will restore health unto thee, and I will heal thee of thy wounds, saith the LORD; because they called thee an Outcast, saying, This is Zion, whom no man seeketh after.

Jeremiah 33:6

> Behold, I will bring it health and cure, and I will cure them, and will reveal unto them the abundance of peace and truth.

Jeremiah 30:17

> For I will restore health unto thee, and I will heal thee of thy wounds, saith the LORD; because they called thee an Outcast, saying, This is Zion, whom no man seeketh after.

Ezekiel 22:30

> And I sought for a man among them, that should make up the hedge, and stand in the gap before me for the land, that I should not destroy it: but I found none.

Ezekiel 36:26

> A new heart also will I give you, and a new spirit will I put within you: and I will take away the stony heart out of your flesh, and I will give you an heart of flesh.

Zechariah 2:5

> Then said I, Whither goest thou? And he said unto me, To measure Jerusalem, to see what is the breadth thereof, and what is the length thereof.

Matthew 6:10

> Thy kingdom come. Thy will be done in earth, as it is in heaven.

Matthew 6:12

> And forgive us our debts, as we forgive our debtors.

Matthew 6:33

> But seek ye first the kingdom of God, and his righteousness; and all these things shall be added unto you.

Matthew 6:13

> And lead us not into temptation but deliver us from evil: For thine is the kingdom, and the power, and the glory, forever. Amen.

Matthew 11:28

> Come unto me, all ye that labour and are heavy laden, and I will give you rest.

Matthew 22:37

> Jesus said unto him, Thou shalt love the Lord thy God with all thy heart, and with all thy soul, and with all thy mind.

Mark 10:8-9

> And they twain shall be one flesh: so then they are no more twain, but one flesh. What therefore God hath joined together, let not man put asunder.

Luke 17:11-16

> And it came to pass, as he went to Jerusalem, that he passed through the midst of Samaria and Galilee. And as he entered into a certain village, there met him ten men that were lepers, which stood afar off: And they lifted up their voices, and said, Jesus, Master, have mercy on us. And when he saw them, he said unto them, go shew yourselves unto the priests. And it came to pass, that, as they went, they were cleansed. And one of them, when he saw that he was healed, turned back, and with a loud voice glorified God, and fell down on his face at his feet, giving him thanks: and he was a Samaritan.

John 1:29

> The next day John seeth Jesus coming unto him, and saith, Behold the Lamb of God, which taketh away the sin of the world.

John 4:24

God is a Spirit: and they that worship him must worship him in spirit and in truth.

John 16:13

Howbeit when he, the Spirit of truth, is come, he will guide you into all truth: for he shall not speak of himself; but whatsoever he shall hear, that shall he speak: and he will shew you things to come.

Romans 12:2

And be not conformed to this world: but be ye transformed by the renewing of your mind, that ye may prove what is that good, and acceptable, and perfect, will of God.

Romans 15:13

Now the God of hope fill you with all joy and peace in believing, that ye may abound in hope, through the power of the Holy Ghost.

1 Corinthians 2:16

For who hath known the mind of the Lord, that he may instruct him? But we have the mind of Christ.

1 Corinthians 12:26-27

And whether one member suffer, all the members suffer
with it; or one member be honoured, all the members
rejoice with it. Now ye are the body of Christ, and
members in particular.

1 Corinthians 14:15

What is it then? I will pray with the spirit, and I will pray
with the understanding also: I will sing with the spirit,
and I will sing with the understanding also.

2 Corinthians 1:20

For all the promises of God in him are yea, and in him
Amen, unto the glory of God by us.

2 Corinthians 10:3-5

For though we walk in the flesh, we do not war after the
flesh: (For the weapons of our warfare are not carnal,
but mighty through God to the pulling down of strong
holds;) Casting down imaginations, and every high thing
that exalteth itself against the knowledge of God, and
bringing into captivity every thought to the obedience
of Christ.

2 Corinthians 13:14

The grace of the Lord Jesus Christ, and the love of God,
and the communion of the Holy Ghost, be with you

all. Amen. (The second epistle to the Corinthians was written from Philippi, a city of Macedonia, by Titus and Lucas.)

Galatians 3:27

For as many of you as have been baptized into Christ have put on Christ.

Galatians 5:16

This I say then, Walk in the Spirit, and ye shall not fulfil the lust of the flesh.

Galatians 6:9

And let us not be weary in well doing: for in due season we shall reap, if we faint not.

Ephesians 1:18

The eyes of your understanding being enlightened; that ye may know what is the hope of His calling, and what the riches of the glory of his inheritance in the saints.

Ephesians 1:22

And hath put all things under his feet, and gave him to be the head over all things to the church.

Ephesians 2: 19-22

> Now therefore ye are no more strangers and foreigners, but fellow citizens with the saints, and of the household of God; And are built upon the foundation of the apostles and prophets, Jesus Christ himself being the chief corner stone; In whom all the building fitly framed together groweth unto an holy temple in the Lord: In whom ye also are builded together for an habitation of God through the Spirit.

Ephesians 4:2-3

> With all lowliness and meekness, with longsuffering, forbearing one another in love; Endeavouring to keep the unity of the Spirit in the bond of peace.

Ephesians 4:23

> And be renewed in the spirit of your mind.

Ephesians 4:32

> And be ye kind one to another, tenderhearted, forgiving one another, even as God for Christ's sake hath forgiven you.

Ephesians 5:21-25

> Submitting yourselves one to another in the fear of God. Wives, submit yourselves unto your own husbands, as unto the Lord. For the husband is the head of the wife, even as Christ is the head of the church: and he is the

saviour of the body. Therefore as the church is subject unto Christ, so let the wives be to their own husbands in everything. Husbands, love your wives, even as Christ also loved the church, and gave himself for it.

Ephesians 5:28

So ought men to love their wives as their own bodies. He that loveth his wife loveth himself.

Ephesians 6:4

And, ye fathers, provoke not your children to wrath: but bring them up in the nurture and admonition of the Lord.

Ephesians 6:12

For we wrestle not against flesh and blood, but against principalities, against powers, against the rulers of the darkness of this world, against spiritual wickedness in high places.

Philippians 2:5a

Let this mind be in you, which was also in Christ Jesus.

Philippians 2:17

Yea, and if I be offered upon the sacrifice and service of your faith, I joy, and rejoice with you all.

Philippians 4:6-8

> Rejoice in the Lord always: and again I say, Rejoice. Let your moderation be known unto all men. The Lord is at hand. Be careful for nothing; but in everything by prayer and supplication with thanksgiving let your requests be made known unto God. And the peace of God, which passeth all understanding, shall keep your hearts and minds through Christ Jesus. Finally, brethren, whatsoever things are true, whatsoever things are honest, whatsoever things are just, whatsoever things are pure, whatsoever things are lovely, whatsoever things are of good report; if there be any virtue, and if there be any praise, think on these things.

Colossians 1:18

> And he is the head of the body, the church: who is the beginning, the firstborn from the dead; that in all things he might have the preeminence.

Colossians 2:7

> Rooted and built up in him, and stablished in the faith, as ye have been taught, abounding therein with thanksgiving.

Colossians 3:2

> Set your affection on things above, not on things on the earth.

Colossians 3:13a

> Forbearing one another, and forgiving one another, if any man have a quarrel against any: even as Christ forgave you, so also do ye.

2 Timothy 1:7

> For God hath not given us the spirit of fear; but of power, and of love, and of a sound mind.

2 Timothy 3:15

> And that from a child thou hast known the holy scriptures, which are able to make thee wise unto salvation through faith which is in Christ Jesus.

Hebrews 8:10

> And that ye put on the new man, which after God is created in righteousness and true holiness.

Hebrews 12:2a

> Looking unto Jesus the author and finisher of our faith; who for the joy that was set before him endured the cross, despising the shame, and is set down at the right hand of the throne of God.

James 4:7-8a

> Submit yourselves therefore to God. Resist the devil, and he will flee from you. Draw nigh to God, and he will draw nigh to you.

James 5:15

> And the prayer of faith shall save the sick, and the Lord shall raise him up; and if he have committed sins, they shall be forgiven him.

1 Peter 1:13

> Wherefore gird up the loins of your mind, be sober, and hope to the end for the grace that is to be brought unto you at the revelation of Jesus Christ.

1 Peter 2:24

> Who his own self bare our sins in His own body on the tree, that we, being dead to sins, should live unto righteousness: by whose stripes ye were healed.

1 Peter 3:7

> Likewise, ye husbands, dwell with them according to knowledge, giving honour unto the wife, as unto the weaker vessel, and as being heirs together of the grace of life; that your prayers be not hindered.

1 Peter 5:7

> Casting all your care upon him; for He careth for you. Be sober, be vigilant; because your adversary the devil, as a roaring lion, walketh about, seeking whom he may devour.

1 Peter 5:10

> But the God of all grace, who hath called us unto his eternal glory by Christ Jesus, after that ye have suffered a while, make you perfect, stablish, strengthen, settle you

1 John 5:4

> For whatsoever is born of God overcometh the world: and this is the victory that overcometh the world, even our faith.

Acknowledgments

First and foremost, I to give reverence, honor, and thank our God, who is the head of my life. It is because of Him I live and move and have my being!!! Nothing is possible without Him in my life. Without the Lord on my side, I am sure I would not be here. I bless the Lord God for such a wonderful loving and supportive husband, Kelvin A. Cox. He has supported me in every Kingdom building assignment and has truly inspired me beyond what words can describe through this whole process to keep pressing towards the mark of completion. Thank you, my Love.

Also, I want to recognize some of the best friends and women of God anyone could ever ask for. My beautiful, amazing, wonderful, and Spirit-filled sisters: Roberta Nettles, Jacqueline Maxwell, Patti Gregory, Pamela Wood, and Minister Evangelist Krista Pettiford. Words will never be able to express how much I love and thank you for all you have poured into my life. Each one of you has inspired me to do and be better. Through it all, we made it Sisters.

And lastly, I want to acknowledge a few of the many others who encouraged me to keep pressing on, I thank you. To name a few: Mother Debra Shaw, Mother Charmayne Collier, Mother Billie Stafford, Mother Vicki Gatewood, Apostle Annette Gatlin, and Lady Naomi Miller. I thank all you wonderful women of God who have labored in prayer with me and have kept me focused. It is my hope and prayer that our Heavenly Father will continue to keep and bless each one of you always.

Humbly,
Brenda Rochelle Cox

To Contact Brenda visit:

Website: https://womenofgodpositionedforpromise.org/
Email: womenofGodpositionedforpromise@gmail.com
Facebook: https://www.facebook.com/
Women-Positioned-for-Promise-1463218767266293/

Printed in the United States
by Baker & Taylor Publisher Services